MW00721199

**Living with stress is a choice
Not a fact of life**

Monty C. Ritchings

Printed by Hignell's Printing Unigraphics
Winnipeg MB
2007

Copyright © 2007 Monty Clayton Ritchings

Catalogue In Print number RA785.R58 2007
155.9042   C2007-904153-1

ISBN Number 978-0-9781891-2-9

Published by Monty C. Ritchings
c/o Dream Chaser Books
#3–2733 Barnet Highway,
Coquitlam, BC Canada V3B 1C2

Graphic Design by Dale Costanzo

Table of Contents

Introduction

Are you feeling stressed out?
Is life getting to be too much?
You are not alone. Stress is rampant throughout all levels of our society. People are becoming seriously ill and dying prematurely because of excessive stress.

It is time to stop. It is time to:
STAMP OUT STRESS

If you look in any library or do a search on the internet, you will find mountains of information on stress. What causes it, what does it do to us? How does it affect our lives and our loved ones? What is stress? Is all stress harmful?

How come if we have all this information, people are still being struck down prematurely? Why are people dying before their time?

When stress is referred to in this book, it is not really the stress that is the concern, it is the attitudes and habits that promote stress, the reactions to stress that are of concern. The stress of normal life is not bad for you; in fact it is good for you. It is the stress promoted through mismanagement of some of life's situations that causes noticeable deterioration of health and quality of life that is of concern.

In this book, we are going to take a very different look at stress. Different because my perspective says that living with stress is a choice, not a fact of life.

You have the choice to be stressed out or you can read this book and learn how to get your life under control, or at least managed in a better way.

I promise you we will not reiterate the stories of old. I will not suggest to you to go to your doctor and get him to prescribe any of a thousand pills to cure you. However, if you are currently under the care of a doctor, counselor or any other health professional, please use this information as an assistance to their good work. My intention is to provide good support for whatever method of healing you are doing. If it is working, please keep going.

My desire for you is to know that you have gained a new understanding of how stress got to be a part of your life. My plan is to enlighten you about my truth about stress and to give you some simple techniques to get your life in order so that stress is what it is supposed to be, not what it currently is in your life.

Am I going to tell you that there will be no stress in your life? Absolutely not. The only time you will know a stress free time is after you have paid your bill and checked out of this great hotel.

What I am going to do is help you to understand how you create stress in your life and how you have let it take over without you even knowing. My goal is to give you back your life, your health, your relationships and the joy of being alive on this planet.

So come on and join me in the journey through this book. Although the message is very serious, I will try to keep this light and fun. After all, this is the way life is supposed to be.

I wish you well with wonderful peace of mind and fullness of life.

Namaste
Monty

Chapter 1:

Where did it all go wrong?

Do you remember when you were a kid? Do you remember those great summer nights hanging around with your buds, not a care in the world?

What happened?

Life did!

All the time you were a child, although you may not have been aware of it, you were busy learning the rules of life. And like most people, those rules you learned way back before your wisdom teeth came in are still hard at work in your life today.

Psychologists say that 90% of the beliefs you have today were created before you saw your seventh birthday. Isn't that wonderful? So what were you doing prior to that glorious day?

How about some of these great pastimes?
- Getting beaten up by the neighbourhood bully
- Watching mom and dad scream at each other
- Learning the multiple uses of belts and straps every time you tried to experience life for yourself
- Trying to get your parents attention and approval so you could feel good about your life
- Hiding from people who tried to hurt you
- Trying to develop new friendships every time mom and dad opted for a great new place to live.
- Skipping school

No matter what happened during childhood, each of us learned that life does not work out the way we thought it would in our mind.

I have often said that something went seriously wrong with my life the day that I was booking my trip on Star Trek's Holideck computer. I thought I was punching in a long term holiday hanging out on the beach in Jamaica enjoying the Caribbean sunsets!

Did I get a rude awakening! I haven't even seen Jamaica this trip!

I finally realized not that long ago that it was not the Holideck computer that screwed up. It was my perception of life! I was trying to run my life based on the rules I had learned as a kid!

The rules I had learned were not realistic for my life now and did nothing for me in helping me to manage my life.

Of course, I was stressed out!

Could you imagine trying to bake a cake when the instructions you have are for making soup? It can not and will not ever work no matter how hard you try!

That is the way we do so much of life! It's no wonder stress is so rampant. We are totally off kilter with our life because we keep trying to live our life based on inaccurate and inadequate information. How can we expect to create a wonderful life when many of the rules we base our life on are actually designed to sabotage us?

Do you think that maybe the same thing has happened to you… and likely everyone else? Is it possible that we are still living on those same old rules that probably didn't even serve us when we were little? And for the most part, we don't even realize what they are doing to our lives? No wonder we are stressed out!

It is not possible to build a healthy life style if we have unhealthy beliefs about ourselves and life in general.

Is there anything we can do about it? Is there any hope for us or for mankind? Are we destined to evaporate as a species due to en masse burnout?

So where did it all go wrong?

Well, this is going to take the whole book to discuss this one. I must forewarn you though, I am a little radical in my view of the world and a whole lot jaded. I am not going to spend very much time explaining the basis of our belief systems as this book is a handbook to get your life back on track right now! If you want to know more about core beliefs and how they impact your life, may I suggest you read my first book:

What Your Mom and Dad Didn't Know They Were Teaching You

It is the pilot book of my Series: *Embracing The Blend.*

Anyway, somewhere back in time, someone thought it would be cute to promote the idea that we had to live our lives according to the demands and desires of other people and other things in our lives just so they could be happy and feel in control.

How many times have we heard that old classic line: "Do it for your mama?"

We bought into it well, so now we spend most of our time trying frantically to pay off mortgages bigger than the national debt of 1938, trying to make support payments for kids and spouses who couldn't take the stress any more and a gazillion other daily activities that have to be dealt with all in the name of living a successful life and keep "mama" happy.

Then when we finally have a few minutes of down time, we zone out by guzzling beer while drowning ourselves in some mindless TV show filled with violence.

I ask you, where is there peace in that?

It's like living in a hamster cage. We get ourselves on that infernal wheel only getting off to feed, breed and die.

If you look at how your parents lived, they never stopped working did they? But who did they do it for?

In reality they did it for themselves. But their rhetoric sounded something like this: "We did all this for you. We worked ourselves to the bone, so you could have the good life… and on and on".

Recognition of this bit of nonsense is the first step in the realization of what went wrong.

We never do things for other people unless the action first has a benefit for us at some level.

Often when people tell you that they are doing things for you, they are just applying a wonderful coating of guilt onto your belief systems as they attempt to keep you in their control. After all, they have become comfortable with whom they see you as, so they will do anything to keep you there in an attempt to protect their comfort zone.

We have learned to live in a manner much like the way some caterpillars did in an experiment a while back. The scientist put a bunch of them around the rim of a glass. The caterpillars thought this was their lot in life so they kept hanging onto the rim. Every time one of these characters started to fall off, their buddies on either end would pull them back up.

Sound familiar? How many times have you been pulled back into your rut by your family, friends, etc.?

What if you wanted your life to go somewhere different than they were comfortable with? What if you were to just let go?

The key to understanding what happened is this:

Somewhere along the line we forgot what we came to this life for. We forgot about being here for the joy and the experience of being alive and free and to decide for ourselves what our life is for.

We traded this knowledge for "feeling safe" by giving away our power to anybody and anything that would take it.

We then covered ourselves even deeper in this muck by allowing our egos to take over our lives and make us believe that accumulating stuff and being bigger than other people is what makes us great and powerful.

Sadly, all we have done is ruined a great time and seriously shortened our life spans.

So, are you with me?

I say we need to have a revolt!

We need to take back our power as individual people and in return we can **STAMP OUT STRESS!**

Chapter 2

What is all this stress doing to us?

We all have our own version of "Survivor" going on. I am not going to get into a bunch of boring statistics. You know what your life is like. No statistic in the world will accurately describe what motivated you to pick this book up.

Rather than numbers and boring statistics, this book is about reality living or more accurately living in reality. The evidence is in our face everyday of our lives. We see the changes happening every time we breathe. Now we need to get back in charge of our lives or we also will be a statistic.

I feel like most people I see in my life are trying to just keep up with all the "stuff" that's going on. Life seems to be about "surviving" rather than living. It seems that life has become like a perpetual speedboat that keeps whipping us along so fast that we feel like we can't jump off for fear of being injured or even killed.

It appears that we are suffocating under this illusion of "having to".

There is less and less time available for having fun and generally relaxing. Without this down time, our bodies and mind have no opportunity to recharge. Our boat is constantly in full speed ahead with little hope of changing course.

So what happens when we live a life of being continually on the go, pressing forward in a relentless effort to make others happy by constantly "doing"?

Later on, I will talk about the body aspect of stressful living. Right now, I would like us to focus on life style concerns. Some of the great complaints about how we live at this time are directly related to this need for constant busyness and the resulting rising tide of stress. They include road rage, the increase in violent crime, emotional and psychological damage to our children and domestic violence along with the increase in the number of divorces and much more.

Just medicate and go!

And of course, we need to look at what we are doing to mother earth. The rise in pollution and general stress on the planet due to our rising demand for consumer goods and the toll that our rising population has taken is a direct result of a planet of people who need to have that void filled from outside their being because they do not take the time to fill it themselves.

Have you noticed the drastic change in weather in the last few years? That is our demand for consumer products that is fueling it. No sense blaming China and India for creating the pollution. If we didn't want the stuff, they wouldn't be making it!

We seem to be obsessed with the need to fill the void inside ourselves with "stuff", just so we can feel good, so we can feel successful. Now I am not advocating that we all go live on communes and draw our water from wells and eat only carrots. I enjoy having a nice car and a beautiful home and lots of other nice things. But I am not willing to die for them! And I know that my survival is not dependant on having them!

It is not the possessions or the desire for them that is the concern; it is the attitude of having to have them to survive that is the problem!

Let's look at our bodies. Much of the foods we eat are manufactured from chemicals rather than plant or animal matter. We microwave our food rather than either cooking it or eating it raw. And to finish it off, we eat it so fast that the food gets broken down by adrenaline rather than digestive juices. Then when our body retaliates, we pop pills to suppress the signals that things are going awry. Is that stress causing?

The average person today gets their exercise from pushing either a pen or a computer mouse around all day followed by a healthy dose of pushing buttons on the television remote at night. Oh sorry, we must also include the elbow bending derived from slurping back several beers each evening. Does that promote peace of mind?

The end result is obesity, high blood pressure, strokes, heart attacks, diabetes, cancer and other diseases manifesting in a lot of unhappy people who die a lot younger than they need to.

So what can we do about it?

Chapter 3

What can we do about it?

Life is about making choices.

We make some choices automatically and we make some through conscious effort.

Life has become so busy now that it seems there is no time for taking a break and making those deliberate choices. Every moment seems to require a new decision being made even though we haven't really decided on the last one yet.

Did you know that we process over double the amount of information today than our parents did at our age? We also live about twice the amount of life in a day than people did a hundred years ago.

It is not difficult to travel many thousands of miles in a twenty-four hour period today. A hundred years ago, most people barely lost site of the town they were born in.

We need to accept that life is not the same as it was generations ago.

At the same time, we also need to understand that our psyche or the mental side of us has not adjusted to the so-called demands of this faster paced life. The result being adaptation to stress by synthetic means such as drugs and alcohol or working until we either have a mental breakdown or just plain old opt out of the game we call life.

I think one of the first things we need to realize is that most of us have taken on a whole lot more in our lives than we can comfortably handle.

We need to admit to ourselves that there are some things in our lives that need to change. I feel we need to also realize that if we do not change them by our own volition, the force of life will change them for us.

We have grown up with a belief that we need to work tirelessly to prove our worth, to keep the image of our parents giving us approval in our heads placated. The truth is:

We are not obligated to do what others want. We have the right to choose for ourselves and create life according to our wants, needs and desires.

The only thing we need to do is give ourselves some space to breathe once in a while we are living our lives.

Just stop and take a breath once in a while!

It is also good for each of us to recognize the noise in our heads; we carry with us that drive us into that state of being out of control. We have become adrenaline junkies. We live to the extreme. We use the "extremeness" of our lifestyle to justify staying unconscious, running from that never ending voice. As long as we can hold onto this "drug", we can avoid ourselves and the responsibility for our lives.

Unfortunately, this would be like continuing to joy ride in a speedboat that has already struck a big rock out in the middle of a lake.

Here's some examples of what I mean:
• We persistently drive our cars too fast
• We drink gallons of coffee when we know we are already "wired"
• We get upset and aggressive when other people don't agree with us
• We constantly have the "latest and greatest" whether we need it or not
• We watch violent television programs

- Our life goal is to be "Number One"
- We live in "perpetual motion" (even in our sleep)
- We think that if we stop, so will our life

In my mind, the whole process of so-called "normal" living has gone berserk. We have lost control of our lives. And we have the audacity to call it living the good life!

What can we do about it?

The first thing we can do is realize that we always have choice.

We can continue to drive the boat right down to the bottom of the lake and drown or we can get to shore and fix it before continuing.

There is no such thing as "have to". We always have choice. It is a matter of whether we will make our choice by rote and carry on as we always have or will we stop and choose to try something different (Hopefully before life forces our hand!).

If we continue making the same decisions we will go down with the boat.

If we decide to choose a different outcome, we are faced with a dilemma, and this is where the fear arises that keeps most people in their rut.

"What if I make the wrong decision?" you ask. Well my friend, would you rather risk making a decision that turns out badly but different or just continue making the same old choice again and again?

In a worst case scenario, you make a decision that still takes you down with the boat, but at least you now know you have tried something different and that alone is a win.

Life is a gamble... but the risk can be limited.

If you take the time to think about what you would like the outcome to be rather than just allowing knee jerk reactions, it is quite likely you will make a decision that is not detrimental. It will likely need fine tuning as the situation rises again. Just know and accept that it will not hurt you if you have made a deliberate and conscious decision.

If you take the time to think about what you would like the outcome to be rather than just allowing knee jerk reactions, it is quite likely you will make a decision that is not detrimental. It will likely need fine tuning as the situation rises again. Just know and accept that it will not hurt you if you have made a deliberate and conscious decision.

Let's look at the first steps in understanding what you can do about getting some control in this stressful life you have created for yourself.

They are:
• Recognize that you are living beyond your manageable limits
• Recognize that you can create a life that is simpler and more manageable simply by making the choice to change your life.

As this little book progresses you will learn several other concepts and tools that will help you retool your life to **STAMP OUT STRESS.**

Chapter 4
How did we learn to do stress?

Everything we have learned in this life has been ingested through watching and interacting with others. In my book *What Your Mom and Dad Didn't Know They Were Teaching You,* I go into much greater detail about the mechanics of how we learn.

For the sake of the simplicity and brevity of this handbook, suffice it to say that we have learned virtually everything we know and all the ways we react to life by watching others.

If you watch a father and son walking down the street, you will notice that they most likely walk in a similar gait. This is because our children learn to walk by watching other people around them walking. The person they feel most similar to or have the strongest affinity with will be the person they emulate in much of what we consider automatic learning.

The son actually learns the process of walking by watching the others around him, and then eventually learns to get up and walk on his own by repeating their actions.

The same thing can be said for how we deal with life situations. If you look at the authority figures (mom, dad, teachers, siblings, etc) in your life and how they have made their choices in various situations, then look at how you do things, you will likely see a common pattern. This is because most people unconsciously learn "the functional method" for dealing with a certain situation and then copying it. This is done completely without any conscious thinking at all!

Some common examples of this could be:
- The words we use to express ourselves, especially in certain situations
- Body gesturing or automatic reactions to certain stimuli
- Activities used to fill your days (television, sports, reading, etc)
- Use of alcohol and drugs
- Driving habits and how we deal with driving situations
- The expression or suppression of emotions
- How we treat other people, especially children and people of the opposite sex

Take a few moments now and look back at your childhood. Think of situations where your caregivers and role models acted out specific situations in their lives. After you have chosen a few scenarios look at how you react in those same situations. Who did you pattern yourself after? Unless you have made some deliberate choices related to certain situations, you can almost always pin your reaction as a copy of one of your caregivers. This is unconscious learning.

This is also true of how we have learned to deal with stress.

As children we literally know nothing about how to deal with life. Our unconscious mind is completely open to suggestion. We watch mom and dad deal with life. Life is one never ending continuum of learning. Stress and dealing with stressful activities in life had no different consideration than learning how to use a toilet or eating with a fork or spoon. The mind does not care about the quality of the information or even what the information is, it only wants information to fill the void.

When reactions to situations repeat again and again over a long period of time, they become ingrained as an acceptable and automatic response to the given situation. This is true even if the result is not beneficial or acceptable to the authority figures or the individual committing the act.

It is really a sad state of affairs when a parent punishes a child for their reaction to a situation when all the child did was copy the parent in their own reaction, and yet it happens time and again, and will continue to recur until conscious change occurs.

But fear not, there is hope!

Chapter 5
What does stress feel like?

One of the first steps in being able to deal with stress and managing it is learning how to recognize how stress feels.

It is amazing how so many people today are not truly in touch with the feel of their body and its actions as it works its way through each day. They are so wrapped up in reacting to life in their own unconscious patterns that they have lost any sense of connection to themselves and therefore do not realize the results until it is too late.

The result from long term disconnection from body awareness is premature breakdown at some or all levels. This might include physically, mentally and/or emotionally. At the end, this person will be less than fully functional or even dead.

Things one can look forward to by remaining in this unconscious process might include:

- Extreme mental fatigue causing an inability to think clearly, or at all
- Mental or emotional breakdowns
- Pretty well any disease
- Uncontrolled outbursts of destructive emotions
- Loss of quality relationships with others
- Lack of true quality lifestyle
- A much shorter life

It is important to be able to recognize the symptoms that indicate stress is active or may be sitting on the sidelines waiting for the opportunity to activate in your life.

I know I promised that I would not get too academic in this book but I feel it is important to understand how stress changes the body functions. I will try to keep it interesting while we tread through these puddles of academia.

Stress is a product of fear.

Fear produces changes in the body that are managed by the Endocrine System. The Endocrine System is composed of any glands that manufacture and/or distribute hormones. Hormones are not only found in the sex glands. Hormones are chemicals which cause change due to stimulus often from an external source.

Adrenaline is a perfect example of what I am talking about. Another one is Insulin.

When a person feels unsafe, their glands produce and excrete hormones in order to excite certain functions in the body so the body is prepared to either fight or run. This is called the "Fight or Flight" Syndrome.

Early recognition is key to managing the situations in your life.

When a situation invokes stress, the body reacts in much the same way as when it is in fear mode. As you live each of you days, try to gain a better sense of the feelings of being in the current emotion, especially when you are feeling stress.

Due to the pace most of us live today, we are continually in a level of stress that is beyond the normal condition that our body functions best at. Therefore, it takes far less to cause an unhealthy reaction.

These are some of the most common physical symptoms:
- Muscle tightness anywhere in the body that is not required for completing the current action, such as tight head muscles causing a head ache, or back pains.
- Pulsing at the end of the nose
- Acidy stomach
- Inability to sit or stand still

- Inability to think clearly, fast moving mind that shifts from one thought to another in very fast rotation
- Difficulty in breathing (Tight chest)
- Rapid heart beat even though not exercising
- Lots of gas from the digestive system
- Tingling hands
- In extreme cases, blurred vision
- Tingling lips

Mental and Emotional Symptoms include:
- An urgent feeling of needing to protect one self
- A feeling of panic
- A sense of feeling overwhelmed
- Inability to let go of a particular thought that keeps recycling in the mind.

These symptoms are commonly experienced when a person is feeling excessive stress. I strongly urge again being aware of these feelings and of other feelings in the body so that you can take appropriate action while they are still manageable and well before they can cause any damage.

We learned to react to life in this manner.
We can retrain ourselves to live differently.

Learn to listen to your body then do something about the messages.

Chapter 6

Mind management is stress management

Now we get down to the business at hand, the reason I put this book together.

Stress is a learned reaction, it is controllable and manageable.

The first step in learning to manage stress in your life is realizing and accepting that you have choice every time you "get stressed out".

You have the choice whether to react in that manner or to respond differently.

The difference, by the way, between "react" and "respond" is the difference between acting out of habit and consciously making a choice.

Learning to manage stress in your life needs to start in the times when you are not feeling stressed.

If you understand well how to manage stress when you are feeling comfortable, it will be much easier for you to manage your life when situations get out of control.

Recognizing the effects of thoughts in your head is absolutely required. This requires being able to separate yourself from the outcome or the reaction. After all,

You are not your thoughts and they are not you.

Being able to differentiate between who you are and the "things" going on in your life is essential for improving your mind and life management.

Please understand that you can not and will never ever have complete control over the events in your life. If you can get you head around this one fact, you will reduce stress in your life immeasurably.

So, this is where the exercises begin. For your benefit I have also provided these exercises on a bookmark and on a CD at the back of the book. Please read through this section first before doing the exercises.

Sit yourself down, get comfortable and begin to relax. As you settle in, take in three very slow easy breaths.

An important note: when you breathe, whether now or anytime, remember to breathe moving your abdominal muscles. This allows your lungs to refresh all of the air in them including at the base of the lungs. If this does not occur, stale air stays in the bottom of the lung and is redistributed through the blood causing a lack of revitalization (which increases stress).

Now pretend there is a warm yellow sun beaming down on you from above your head. As you continue to breathe in a very slow deliberate manner, feel the warmth of the sun flowing down into your body.

Feel it flow down your head, your neck, into your chest, down into your abdomen and down your legs, flowing right down into your feet. Take your time and let yourself relax.

Feel your feet firmly planted on the ground. Focus on this feeling for a good moment, then let your consciousness move back up your body from your feet, up your legs into your pelvic region, up into your abdomen, through your chest, into your neck and up to the top of your head.

Once you have done this action as many times as you desire, allow yourself to relax fully into your chair and feel the connection between your bottom and the chair.

Focus on your breaths and the feeling of being in your body. Let yourself feel every part of your body from head to toe. Allow yourself to enjoy the feeling.

Every time you catch yourself thinking about something else, gently pull yourself back into focusing on your body and breath.

This is practicing being in the NOW. Feeling the sensations of being in your body, along with giving attention to your breath is a route for maintaining contact with present time.

Allow yourself to be aware of any feelings in your body. Make allowances for any sounds and smells in the room and just let them be. They belong in the present. Thoughts that distract your practice do not belong, so gently dismiss them.

Most important, be easy on yourself. Let yourself relax. When you are ready to finish up, just take a nice easy breath and open your eyes.

Practice this exercise every day. Practice it when you are feeling calm.

Teach yourself to remember how it feels to be conscious of your body and breath in present time. This provides you with an anchor for when the times are hectic.

Keeping your mind present in the now allows you to stay out of old habits and make better decisions.

Remember, when you take the time to make good decisions for yourself, the results are good for others in the long run.

Chapter 7

Managing your thoughts

Definitely the biggest challenge in keeping yourself managed and at peace is dealing with the noise in your head. Fortunately, there are several key pieces of information available that will help you to gradually take the driver's seat in mind management.

Definitely practicing the exercise in the previous chapter is a basic part of creating change in your life and gaining more peace of mind.

Next is understanding that stress is a choice.

Stress is a result of poor management of your thoughts.

You see, most people do not understand that thoughts are manageable. The mind is no different than any other tool. The only difference is that we are not generally taught that we can do anything about stress or anything else that goes on in our head except tolerate it or medicate it.

As you will soon understand, neither of these solutions are necessary.

Please realize: **You are not your mind, your thoughts or your ego.**

These three are only tools that are implanted inside your being for your benefit. As such, their function and purpose is commonly and severely misunderstood. Let me explain.

Your mind is a very powerful tool. In fact, computers are designed after our brain/mind relationship and work exactly the same way. Like computers, the mind can be turned off and on at will and the information in it can be managed. It just takes practice.

Your thoughts are the information processed by your mind.

Thoughts by themselves have no power.

Thoughts require input from your emotional body in order to activate.

Generally thoughts that promote stress are just rehashed thoughts from your childhood dressed up as adults. They likely were not based on correct information when you were a child and are still just as erroneous today. However, they are the information your mind (computer) knows and therefore bases its reactions from.

In many therapies today, the desire is either to have the client work through the emotional upheaval or medicate in order to suppress the thoughts. The process you are going to learn will teach you how to turn the undesirable thought off by taking away its power. You will also learn to give more "juice" to beneficial thoughts. This is the basis of what I call mind management. Off with the "bad" and on with the "good".

Your ego is one of the most misdirected organs in your body. We are conditioned to believe, in this society, that we are our egos. We do not differentiate between who we truly are and the persona we see through our ego. Because of this belief, the ego is given far more power than it is due.

The ego is an important part of our total self but it is no more important than any other organ in our body. It has a specific purpose just like the brain, liver, kidneys, etc.

The purpose of the ego is to carry our identity around and to be the base of our intuition for survival. In days of old when we needed to rely on our intuition, we needed to have a good awareness of everything going on around us. If we didn't, we would quickly become an involuntary part of the food chain.

The ego's purpose is to protect us, to keep us alive. The ego is found in the subconscious mind. It has no ability to

discern right from wrong. It only knows what it knows. It tries to regulate its owner's life according to what it "knows". Unfortunately, this information is often wrong.

What I am trying to tell you is this:
Much of the stress in your life is caused by your subconscious mind trying to make your life conform to its perception of life.

How unrealistic is that? Is your life the same as it was when you were six years old? Of course it isn't! Did you really understand the full scope of life when you were six? Did those beliefs even serve you well as a child? Of course not! Usually they just happened... and got you into more trouble and they are likely still getting you into trouble!

So what can you do about it?
Learn to manage your mind.

The next step is to allow a thought which stimulates stress to surface in your mind. Allow yourself to feel how the thought affects you. Let your mind travel throughout your body determining how the thought has impacted any part. Can you feel certain muscles being held tight? Do you feel any anxiety? How is your breathing? What is happening in your mind? Are there any other changes from your normal peaceful condition?

Now focus again on your breathing. Slowly take long breaths giving all of your attention to the breath. Remember how it felt to be fully in your relaxed body. Follow the breathing pattern back into the peaceful body.

Allow your mind to go into a stress related thought again, then follow your breathing back into peace and relaxation. You are making conscious choice to move out of one thought into another.

If you are a visual person, this is the technique.

See a chair in the back of your head. It is facing towards your forehead. Sit down in the chair. At the front of your head is a white screen like a movie theatre screen.

As you are sitting in the chair, allow your thoughts to appear on the screen. Try to watch them much like you are watching a movie.

As a stressful thought comes up, melt it like an ice cream cone in the heat of summer. Each time the thought comes up, melt the thought again.

Using either of these processes allows you to regain control over your thoughts. This is mind management. You are becoming the boss. With practice you will be able to neutralize any thought you choose so that you can maintain the level of control you desire.

Chapter 8

The power of mind management

Now that you have the ability and the power to delegate power to whichever thoughts you choose, you can take this to an even higher level.

This next step allows you to stimulate the higher, more desirable thoughts in a similar process to the neutralizing one of the last chapter.

Why would you want to do this?

Nature abhors a void and so does your mind. The ultimate outcome of this process is to have your mind doing exactly what you desire.

Therefore we must look at the elimination or neutralizing of the stressful thoughts as only one aspect of totally conditioning your mind.

One of the benefits of learning the neutralizing technique is that you can allow your mind to come to rest, even to the point where your mind will not have any thought in it at all.

This effect may only last for a few seconds at first but as you practice and become okay with not having to be constantly thinking, your mind will remain in this state of passiveness for several moments or longer.

In yogic terms, this is the state of Nirvana, total peace.

In this space, your mind is not inactive or stopped, it is only resting. In this space you leave room for rejuvenation and inspiration. It is vital to your health and progress on your life journey.

As you practice these exercises, allow yourself the pleasure of enjoying the quiet. It is truly one of the greatest gifts we can give ourselves today.

These exercises, by the way, only need to take 5–10 minutes. They should be done regularly at least once per day. However, in stressful times, please stop and go into the quiet as often as necessary until your are able to return to a reasonable level of calm.

Please note that these exercises are designed to help you live life more fully. They are not meant as an escape from responsibility.

Life will continue to present challenging times and in some cases, it will seem like a never ending barrage. By learning to anchor yourself from within and manage your mind, you will be able to develop a much healthier approach to moving through the issue as they express in your life.

Once the emotion has been removed from the thoughts, you will soon be able to view them in a detached manner and learn what the basis of the thought pattern is, so that you can deal with the message rather than the onslaught of the emotional riptide.

It is part of being human that we have these emotional upheavals. The purpose of this program is to provide you with tools to move through them more quickly, to return you to calm.

Accepting that these situations occur now and will occur again in the future is part of the flavour of life will make it much easier to ride them through.

Now, onto the next part of the exercise.

As I said before, there needs to be balance in the mind management process, therefore we need to counter the neutralizing of the undesirable stress related thoughts.

This is done by reinforcing the desirable thoughts.

Mind management has two components:
Neutralize the undesirable and Reinforce the desirable.

So let's learn how to reinforce the desirable.

Again, close your eyes and relax by taking a few slow deep breaths. This time choose a thought which you deem to be desirable. It could be something you desire or even just a feeling of well-being or it could be a picture of someone or something you have in your life that brings to you feelings of pleasure, gratitude or joy.

Feel how you feel as you allow this thought to permeate your mind. What changes in your body do you feel? How is your breathing?

If you are a visual, you can repeat the process in your head with the chair and the blank screen. This time, however, you choose a desirable thought. Allow it to come up on the screen. Keep it there, enjoy it.

Now, project energy from your heart to the thought. Revel in the joy of having that which you see on the screen.

Decide for yourself what emotion you wish to attach to this thought. Send this emotion into the thought and allow yourself to really enjoy the connection.

Next, and most important, is own the feelings you have created. Allow them to exist in your life in PRESENT tense. Allow yourself to enjoy them, embellish them and make them grow. The more intensity in the feeling, the more your mind will remember it.

No matter what the positive thought, you must attach emotion to it so that the subconscious mind learns to know the experience of positively injected emotions and feelings. By regularly practicing this process, your mind will be reconditioned to feed on positive, desirable energy rather than the old stuck low energy it formerly knew that promotes stress.

This process will retrain the mind to search for and accept positive healthy energy. This stimulates the endocrine system in a beneficial manner.

It is important to understand that your mind needs to be fed and will always be fed through the energy you attract into your body through your thinking. By focusing on and learning to manifest positive stimulating energy through focused thought, you create a life that is more dynamic, resourceful, abundant and healthy.

Although activities that stimulate old memories are unavoidable in life, it is how you choose to allow them to impact your present time through your emotions that makes the difference. You can choose to allow the unconscious mind to wreak havoc in your life and bowl over your health and dreams or you can take charge by reconditioning your mind so that you have conscious control over the programming and the outcomes.

There are no instances in life where you cannot maintain some level of control through mind management. Remember that it has taken you all of your life so far to learn to react to stress in the old way, it will take practice and time to instill this new way of responding to life's influences.

All you have to do is remember yourself and remember you always have a choice in how you let outside influences affect your life.

And most especially important:
Always remember to be your own best friend.

As you retrain your mind, give yourself the space to adjust to the new way. Appreciate yourself for making the effort on a continual basis. Love yourself for the wonderful being that you are. Learn to know the joy of feeling the feeling of being you in your own energy and vitality. By making this effort for yourself, you are helping to make the world a better place to live for everyone.

Namaste

About The Author

Monty Ritchings specializes in helping people understand what drives them. For over thirty years Monty has been a practicing energetic healing facilitator and a medical intuitive, core belief counselor and teacher of programs that assist people in understanding their own inner self.

Monty's first book, *What Your Mom and Dad Didn't Know They Were Teaching You* was released in November 2006.

www.powerofsafety.com

QUICK ORDER FORM

Please check your local book store first. If **Stamp Out Stress** is not available, then please contact us through one of these media.

You can:

- Fill out this page and fax it to: 604-941-3655
- Telephone orders: 604-941-3755
- Email orders to: *info@dreamchaserbooks.com*
- Mail this page to:

  Dream Chaser Books

  #3–2733 Barnet Highway

  Coquitlam, BC Canada V3B 1C2

- Through the Power People Network website: *www.powerpeoplenetwork.net*
- Through the book website: *www.powerofsafety.com*

Ordering Information

Name _____

Address _____

City _____ Province/State_____ Postal code _____

Telephone Number _____ Email address _____

Please send me ____ copies of **Stamp Out Stress**

Charge my credit card for the total amount at $16.95 US or $19.95 CA plus shipping and handling. Receipt of payment will be included with the shipment

Credit card: (please circle type) Visa MasterCard

Card Number _____ Expiry Date _____

Name on Card: _____

For more information regarding the Power People Network, please visit our website
www.powerpeoplenetwork.net
Thank you for your order